H A B I T A T S

A JOURNEY IN NATURE

by Hannah Pang   *Illustrated by Isobel Lundie*

For my smiley baby Willow,
who made a home of me while I wrote this ~ H.P.

To Zulf, who can make me feel home anywhere ~ I.L.

360 DEGREES, an imprint of Tiger Tales
5 River Road, Suite 128, Wilton, CT 06897
Published in the United States 2024
Originally published in Great Britain 2024
by Little Tiger Press Limited
Text by Hannah Pang
Text copyright © 2024, Little Tiger Press Limited
Illustrations copyright © 2024, Isobel Lundie
ISBN-13: 978-1-944530-41-9
ISBN-10: 1-944530-41-X
Printed in China
LIO/1800/0490/0923
2 4 6 8 10 9 7 5 3 1

www.tigertalesbooks.com

The Forest Stewardship Council® (FSC®) is a global, not-for-profit organization
dedicated to the promotion of responsible forest management worldwide.
FSC® defines standards based on agreed principles for responsible forest
stewardship that are supported by environmental, social, and economic
stakeholders. To learn more, visit www.fsc.org

FSC
www.fsc.org
MIX
Paper | Supporting
responsible forestry
FSC® C020056

Nature is like a magical journey that transforms with every step.

Travel to **Borneo's Rain Forests**, which offer a lush and humid habitat to some very noisy residents! Then brave the **Namib Desert**— a dry, barren landscape where many have set up home.

In the **Pacific Ocean** you'll find animals living in some of the deepest, darkest waters on Earth. While the **Black Forest** in Germany— a dark, mystical place—is a haven for many woodland creatures.

You'll find wildlife thriving in the harshest conditions, from the top of the **Andes Mountains** to the windswept moors below, while the warm **Natural Springs** of Florida are the perfect place for animals to laze and lounge.

Open the pages of this stunning book to discover the changing face of nature . . . .

INCREDIBLE RAIN FOREST

The vast island of **Borneo** is famous for its tropical **rain forests,** which are home to an amazing world of wildlife. Travel down from the tops of the trees to see its **wonders** appear.

EMERGENT LAYER

At the top of towering trees, settling fog provides water for the creatures and plants at the roof of the forest.

The **yellow meranti tree** has lightweight seeds that spin like helicopters all the way to the forest floor.

Giant honeybees build their nests far off the ground in the **tualang tree**, also known as "the tree of swarming bees."

The **long-tailed parakeet** is a very sociable animal that sometimes lives in a flock of thousands!

Dawn bats travel many miles to feed on pollen and nectar from plants that flower during the night.

CANOPY

We are now under the roof of the rain forest, where animals are protected from threats up above but can still escape from predators below.

The **orangutan** is the largest tree-living mammal in the world! A baby will cling to its mother and travel with her for the first years of its life.

The **Bornean slow loris** can only be seen at night. It licks toxic glands under its arms to deliver a venomous bite.

The **atlas moth** is a giant in the insect world, with a wingspan as big as a dinner plate!

To save their colony from attack, female **exploding ants** detonate—spraying poisonous yellow goo!

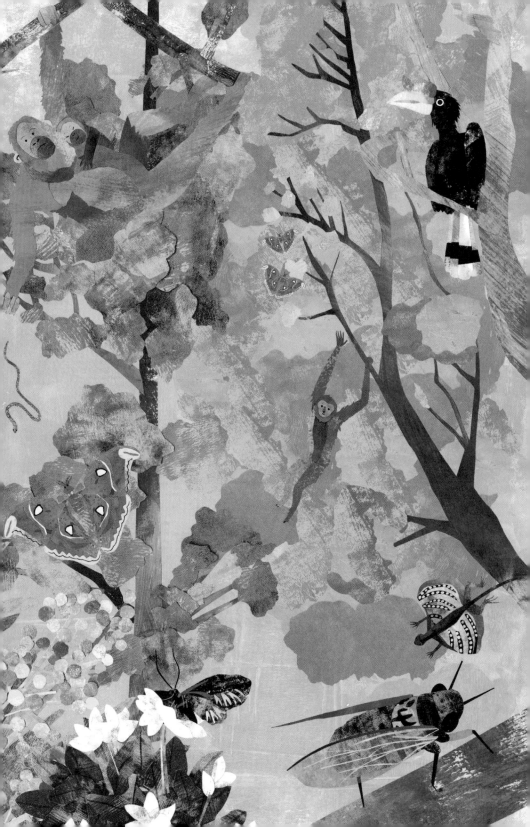

UNDERSTORY

Now we journey down toward the river.
Very little light reaches here, so many plants
grow large leaves to soak up any sun.

The male **proboscis monkey**'s nose is so large that, at times, he has to push it out of the way before he can eat.

The **Bornean spiderhunter** has a long, curved beak for drinking nectar and hooking spiders from webs.

The world's largest flower belongs to the **Rafflesia arnoldii** plant. It smells like rotten meat to attract flies and other insects, which pollinate it.

The **tiger leech** feeds on the blood of mammals, including humans! It moves quickly, delivering a painful bite.

The **giant dead leaf mantis** appears to have a large "eye" on its wings. This makes it look like a much bigger animal, and frightens away predators.

SUNLIT ZONE

The Great Barrier Reef is one of the seven natural wonders of the world. Visible from outer space, it is home to thousands of different species.

Despite looking like a plant, **coral** is actually made up of a group of tiny animals that are related to sea jellies!

The **humphead wrasse** is a huge help to the reef as it feeds on the **crown-of-thorns sea star**—destroyers of coral.

Scientists recently found a bright pink **reef manta ray** near the Great Barrier Reef—the only one discovered in the world!

TWILIGHT ZONE

The twilight zone is sandwiched between the sunlit shallows and the pitch-black deep—and scientists know less about this mysterious zone than the surface of the moon!

Zooplankton are tiny sea animals. They stay in deeper, darker waters during the day to avoid being seen by predators, then move up to the surface at night to feed on microscopic sea plants.

The **Dana lanternfish** lights up to communicate with other lanternfish, and so that predators cannot make out its silhouette.

The **giant siphonophore** is made up of many creatures all joined together, and has a curtain of deadly, stinging tentacles!

The **pelican eel** uses its huge mouth to scoop up fish, shrimp, and plankton. The end of its tail has a flashing light, either to confuse prey or to help it communicate with other eels.

Some **comb jellies** are colorless and almost transparent, except for their guts, which are red. This hides what they've eaten from predators, as the color red can't be seen in deep, dark water.

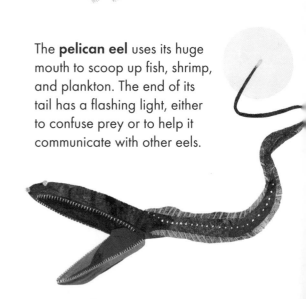

ROCKY SCREE

The animals that live on these slippery rocks seem quite at home among this difficult terrain.

The **southern viscacha** spends its day sunbathing, grooming, or resting. It lives in a group and shelters in rock crevices.

The **black-chested buzzard-eagle** defends its chicks by chasing and attacking any intruders that come too close!

Charles Darwin (an English scientist who studied nature) may have discovered the **Darwin's slipper flower** during his voyage around South America nearly 200 years ago.

LAKESIDE

Breathe, stand back, and take a moment to admire the view by the turquoise waters of Lake Pehoé.

Travel northwest and you might see a **glacier**—an impressive mass of thick ice, sometimes many thousands of years old.

The **Patagonian dragon** is an insect that spends its life on the glacier ice. Antifreeze in its blood means it can survive!

During flight, **Chilean flamingos** communicate with loud, goose-like honks, which help keep the flock together.

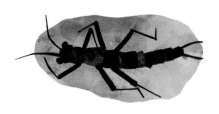

Patagonian pea flowers are also known as sweet peas. But their seeds are not so sweet! In fact, they can be poisonous if eaten in large amounts.

The male **Darwin's rhea** incubates eggs and raises chicks all by himself—the chicks even sleep under his wings for the first couple of months.

INTO THE BLUE

Do not be fooled by the clear, warm spring—many predators lie beneath the sun-dappled water!

The **sailfin armored catfish** attach themselves to manatees and eat the algae that grows on their backs.

The **North American manatee** breaks wind to help it sink! It holds gas in its stomach to float, then lets it out to sink back down.

A top predator, the **American alligator** can be spotted on land, basking in the warm rays of the sun.

Insects are the **six-spotted fishing spider**'s main diet. But it also taps its front legs on the water to attract fish, then dives down to catch them.

The **Florida red-bellied turtle** often lays its eggs in alligator nests to keep them warm. The female alligators protect the eggs from predators, such as raccoons!

The **great blue heron** can bend its neck into an S-shape. It strikes out quickly at fish and frogs—which it swallows whole—and folds up its neck neatly when it flies.

Florida's springs are alive with animals and activity. They're an ideal place for land and water-dwellers alike.

FOREST FLOOR

We reach the forest floor as night falls, although it remains dark down here even during the day.

The **Malayan civet** produces a smelly scent from its bottom when it is threatened. It also uses this to communicate with other civets!

The **greater mouse-deer** is one of the smallest living hoofed mammals, about the size of a large rabbit.

The **Sunda pangolin** is covered in scales and protects its soft, scale-free tummy by rolling up into a ball.

It's believed that **bioluminescent mushrooms** attract light-loving insects. The mushroom spores stick to the insects—who spread them around to create even more mushrooms!

Male **atlas beetles** have horns on their heads to fight other males. The battles take place high in the trees—with the losers stumbling down to the ground.

Rain forests cover only a tiny fraction of the Earth, but are home to more than half of all plant and animal life. It is so important that we take good care of them!

DRY DESERT

The animals and
plants that live
in the world's
oldest desert
rely on the damp fog
that blows in
from the coast of
southwestern
Africa.
Welcome to the
Namib.

SHIFTING DUNES

In this ever-changing landscape, animals emerge to sip moisture from the plants in the coolest moments of the day. Behold some of the tallest sand dunes on Earth!

The **head-stander beetle** sticks its bottom in the air to collect water droplets that it can drink.

When the desert cools, the **Namaqua chameleon**'s body darkens to absorb more heat from the sun. Its body lightens again when it's hot to bounce back the rays and cool itself down.

The **nara melon plant** provides much-needed food and shelter for many animals.

The **golden wheel spider** has a nifty way of escaping predators— it cartwheels down the dunes!

Also known as a "dune shark," the **Grant's golden mole** "swims" through the loose, dry sands, searching for termites to eat. It's nocturnal so is rarely seen.

BARREN PLAINS

This vast open space is full of life but can also be a deadly hunting ground.

The **bat-eared fox** uses its large ears to listen for underground termites, before digging them up as a tasty treat.

Mostly known as scavengers, **spotted hyenas** are also excellent predators. Sometimes they hunt together to bring down springbok and even wild horses, if their pack is big enough.

A group of **meerkats** is called a "mob." The meerkats work as a team to keep watch, gather food, and take care of their young.

Harvester termites collect dead plant matter all through the day and night— they never sleep!

No more than 150 **Namib-Desert horses** roam the dry plains. These rare horses are not native to the country of Namibia, and no one is quite sure how they got there!

The **black hairy thick-tailed scorpion** gets extra moisture from eating reptiles, mice, spiders, and insects—but can survive for up to a year without food!

Rain rarely falls and rivers rarely flow, yet many creatures survive on the few plants that provide shelter, food, and dew in the beautiful Namib.

MYSTERIOUS OCEAN

In every layer

of the ocean,

magical creatures

make their home.

Take a trip off the

eastern coast of

Australia to discover

its many hidden

depths.

ABOVE WATER

The coast, where land meets sea, is a hive of activity as seabirds catch fish with clamorous calls!

The thieving **white-bellied sea eagle** snatches fish from other birds with its huge talons!

The **sailfin flying fish** has a body shaped like a torpedo to pierce through the water's surface—while its large, wing-like fins keep it in the air.

The **silver gull** makes its nest out of seaweed, plant roots, and stems. It's the most common gull in Australia.

DEEP SEA

There is no light in the deepest ocean, and no plants can grow. So in the darkest depths, all of the animals are predators or scavengers.

The **black swallower** has a stretchy stomach, which means it can swallow fish more than twice its length!

Sea pigs gather in huge numbers to feed on decaying matter. They are Nature's vacuums, cleaning up unreachable depths of the ocean.

The tiny male **Krøyer's deep-sea anglerfish** latches onto the much larger female to reproduce. He becomes completely connected to her skin, while his eyes and internal organs dissolve!

Normal bones would crush under the pressure of the water above, but the **hadal snailfish** has a soft skeleton that withstands the force, even on the deepest seabed!

Tardigrades are microscopic animals that can survive boiling hot springs, freezing temperatures, and even outer space—so the high pressures of the deep ocean are no problem!

The **faceless cusk eel** doesn't appear to have a face—but if you look very closely, you might just see one of its tiny eyes.

Hot springs on the seabed, called **hydrothermal vents**, pump out hot water containing minerals into the cold, deep sea.

From the warm shallows to the deepest, darkest depths, ocean animals are some of the most weird and wonderful creatures on Earth.

ANCIENT WOODS

Welcome to the

Black Forest

in Germany—

a wooded mountain

range where ancient,

gnarled trees

block out much

of the sun's light.

These **dark woods**

have inspired many

fairy tales.

IN THE BURROW

As dawn breaks, many of the animals are tucking themselves in after a night of foraging for food.

Badgers often share their setts with rabbits and **red foxes**. But the foxes sometimes upset the badgers with their mess and may be forced to move out!

The poisonous **fly agaric mushroom** has a network of threads beneath the ground. These threads supply trees with nutrients, in exchange for the trees' sugar.

The **cuckoo** is famous for laying its eggs in the nests of other birds. It is more often heard than seen.

The **giant earthworm** can grow to the length of two long rulers placed end to end! It makes a hearty meal for foxes and owls.

Despite its little legs, the **hedgehog** can travel more than a mile on a night-time forage! It snacks on bugs, such as beetles and worms, before returning to its nest to sleep.

THE CLEARING

The sun begins to rise as we leave the deep, dark woods. And a myriad of wildlife awakens.

The **barn owl** is a graceful hunter, gliding silently through the air with specially-shaped wings that make no sound.

The **peregrine falcon** is the fastest bird in the world! When diving toward prey, it makes its body into the shape of a torpedo.

The **Eurasian pygmy owl** is the smallest owl in Europe. It could sit in the palm of your hand!

The venomous **common European adder** will deliver a painful bite if threatened. It can be identified by the dark zigzag pattern running along its body.

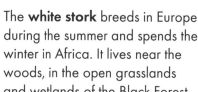

The **white stork** breeds in Europe during the summer and spends the winter in Africa. It lives near the woods, in the open grasslands and wetlands of the Black Forest.

The **great spruce bark beetle** damages spruce trees by tunneling into the bark to lay its eggs. The hatching larvae feed on the inner wood, sometimes killing the tree.

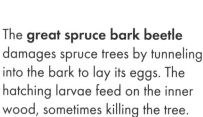

Wild garlic is often found growing in ancient woodlands— it's a sign that you are standing in a rare and special habitat.

The legendary Black Forest is a home to many incredible creatures, fast, slow, big, and small.

MAJESTIC MOUNTAINS

The Andes

is home to

some **rare** and

beautiful wildlife.

This stunning

mountain

range runs all

the way along

South

America's

western side.

MOUNTAIN PEAKS

The rocky mountain tops glow magnificently in the early morning sun. But these spiky granite spires are blustery with freezing winds.

Tectonic plates are vast pieces of the Earth's surface that connect together like a jigsaw puzzle. The **Andes Mountains** were formed over millions of years, when one plate slowly slipped under another.

The **Andean condor** is a large vulture, which circles the sky looking for dead creatures to eat.

The longest feathers on a bird's wing are called **primary feathers**. These are essential for flight.

MOORLAND

Many animals thrive in the harsh, windswept habitat of open moorland, where predators seek out prey in the low-level light.

The **guanaco** has thick skin on its neck to help protect it from the sharp bite of a predator!

The **puma** usually travels alone, stalking its favorite prey of guanacos.

Geoffroy's cat is only seen at night. Its kittens will stay with their mother for around eight months.

As well as spraying a foul smell when threatened, the **Humboldt's hog-nosed skunk** stands up on its hind legs and slams its front paws to the ground while hissing.

The brightly colored **Chilean firebush** attracts insects and birds, which help to pollinate it.

From blustery peaks to sweeping moorland, the Andes presents plenty of challenges— yet many amazing animals thrive in this harsh environment.

NATURAL SPRINGS

The **warm** waters of Florida's natural springs flow from underground to create **winter refuges** for many creatures. Some journey here to **escape** the **cold** rivers and oceans.

SCRUBLAND

The trees and shrubs provide a haven for nocturnal animals, or daytime cover for those that need to stay close to water.

The **Virginia opossum** only comes out at night, and is famous for "playing possum": When threatened by a predator, it lies on the ground and pretends to be dead.

Bald cypress trees sometimes grow woody "knees" that poke up through the ground. These help to anchor the trees into any soft soil.

Despite its armor plating, the **nine-banded armadillo** can swim well, holding its breath for up to six minutes when underwater!

Raccoons have an incredible sense of touch, which helps them to find food. They are often seen at night, dipping their paws into water in search of prey.

From **mountaintops**
to **forest** floors,

from vast **oceans**

to shifting **sands**—

animal habitats

connect together into

one **amazing** home.

Our home.

Our Earth.